All inquiries should be addressed to:
Barron's Educational Series, Inc.
250 Wireless Boulevard
Hauppauge, New York 11788
http://www.barronseduc.com

International Standard Book No. 0-7641-1188-4
Library of Congress Catalog Card No. 99-64273

Printed in Hong Kong
9 8 7 6 5 4 3 2 1

Contents

Why Train Your Dog?

Owning a well-trained dog, one that is welcome everywhere you go, is something to be proud of. However, a dog cannot teach himself. He is dependent on his owner not only for love and care, but also for encouragement and direction to shape his behavior.

Bad habits are easily established and soon become an everyday occurrence. A bad habit is usually a way of behaving that has not been controlled—and before long, you end up with a dog that is blamed for his undesirable, antisocial behavior.

If you decide to own a dog, you must be prepared to take on the task of training, which is a process that continues throughout a dog's life.

A dog's behavior must be shaped by his owner.

efore You Start

ink carefully
fore making your
oice. If you opt
r a registered,
rebred dog, find
t as much as
ssible about the
ed's traits and
aracteristics. Too
ny people
rchase a dog
cause they have
mired a friend's

Consider how much time you can give to training your dog.

ll-behaved pet, or they have seen a
rticular breed competing in Obedience,
ility, or Sheepdog trials, little
lizing how much effort has gone
o achieving the end result.
f you decide on a cross-breed, or an
lt dog from a rescue shelter, it is
re difficult to predict how your dog
l turn out. Mixed parentage can
duce a wonderful dog, but you can
y make a guess when it comes to
essing adult size and character. The
cued dog may have experienced
uma in his early life, and therefore
ert handling and training could be
uired.

*dience Champions make it all look easy,
t never underestimate the effort that has
one into achieving this level of success.*

3

First and foremost try to "think dog," and avoid attributing human feelings or emotions to your pet. Your dog will see you as another dog and will react accordingly.

The dog is a social animal; he enjoys company, especially group activities such as playing and hunting. He needs and enjoys physical contact through touch, grooming, and cuddles.

Dogs communicate through body postures and facial expressions. This "language" can be used as a basis for training and understanding canine behavior.

Your dog will be happier if you make you desires clear and establish household rules that he respects and adheres to. There no need to shout or bully to achieve good results. Training is a continuous learning process that takes time and patience.

Learn how to "think dog

ey Points

Training should be an enjoyable experience
r you and your dog.
Sessions should be short. Little and often is
e best approach.
Learn to read your dog's facial
pressions and body posture; this will
lp you to interpret his attitude or
tentions in different situations.
f you reward good behavior, there is
good chance it will be repeated.
gnore unacceptable behavior, and
is likely to decrease.

pecial Needs

you have chosen an adult dog from
escue center, or have rehomed
log through a breed rescue
ganization, the dog will
obably have some established
utines and behavior patterns that
y take time to reveal themselves.
ith time, understanding, and some
lirectional training, the outcome can
l be extremely
varding.

*Understand your
dog by observing
body posture and
facial expression.*

*A dog from a rescue
shelter will need
special consideration.*

The Right Start

House Rules

It is important to be consistent with your dog. All members of the household should be encouraged to adopt the same attitude and approach. Decide beforehand on the standard of behavior you wish to achieve from your dog and what you will, and will not, allow.

All families have their own "rules," but unacceptable habits usually include jumping up, mouthing/biting, excessive barking, stealing, begging from the table, or letting your dog climb on furniture.

The dog is a pack animal. It is important for your dog that you adopt the role of leader and make the rules as clear as possible. A dog that is allowed to take control will behave like a spoiled child. He will demand to be the center of attention at all times, and he will soon become a nuisance.

arly Learning

oncentration is the basis of all dog training. Dogs are
ually quick to learn their name and simple commands
ch as "Come." The next stage is to work on obedience
ercises such as Sit, Down, and Stay.

Keep training sessions short (five to ten minutes at a time),
d teach one command at a
ne. This will avoid any
nfusion in your
g's mind.
od behavior
ould be
warded with a
od treat, a game
th a favorite toy, or
ving physical or
rbal praise.

he Right Tone

fective use of your voice, and accurate timing of
mmands and praise, will help your dog to learn quickly.
ror-free learning is the key to success.

Listen to your voice. Does it sound cheerful and genuine?
emember, training should be fun for both you and your
ppy.

Practice getting the tone right. Women find the deeper,
ern voice of disapproval difficult to achieve. Men, on the
her hand, find the lighter, more encouraging tone needed
r praise more difficult or embarrassing.

The first rule of dog training is: Do not be self-conscious!
hibited body language or a subdued tone of voice means a
ock in communication and understanding.

The Right Start

Bad Habits

A mistake often made by first-time dog owners is the expectation that as a puppy matures he will stop behaving badly. In reality, bad behavior becomes an established pattern that becomes increasingly difficult to break.

A puppy uses his mouth to investigate new things, and this can lead to excessive mouthing or biting. Right from the start discourage your puppy if he bites your hands or clothes. The best plan is to offer a substitute—a favorite toy—and this will distract him from further biting. Make sure you and your family always follow this procedure, and encourage visitors to do the same.

The natural instincts demonstrated by some breeds can develop into unacceptable behavior. For example, the herding breeds (particularly Border Collies) will often chase traffic. Gundogs (such as Labrador Retrievers and Golden Retrievers) have a strong sense of smell, and this can lead to poor recalls. The digging and ratting tendencies of some Terrier breeds (such as the Jack Russell) may give a gardener a few nightmares. So try to learn as much as you can about the natural instincts of your chosen breed to prevent problems from developing.

A strong sense of smell is an asset in a working dog, but it can lead to poor recalls if a pet dog is allowed to use his nose unchecked.

Collie types often have a strong chasing instinct that must be curbed.

Your puppy must be taught right from wrong from the start. It is not necessary to shout; your dog has an acute sense of hearing, and, in most cases, he will be responsive and willing to please. Discipline should be in the form of:

Disapproval—using a firm, low tone of voice.
Distraction—diverting your dog's attention.
Control—attaching the collar and lead/long line (see page 20).
Indifference—deny your puppy attention while he is displaying unacceptable behavior.

The desire to dig, in breeds like the Jack Russell, can wreak havoc in your garden.

Socialization

The importance of early socialization is widely recognized as a formative factor in developing a sound temperament. In fact, it is often lack of socialization that is the cause of behavioral problems seen in some adult dogs rehomed from rescue shelters.

A puppy needs time to settle into his new home and to get used to the sights and sounds of everyday living.

Broadening Horizons

As your puppy becomes accustomed to your home, broaden his experiences. Make short trips in the car to friends' home or, if he is a small dog, carry him around the block. Allow him to see and hear traffic and groups of strangers but, to assure his good health, be sure he isn't exposed to other dogs until his puppyhood vaccinations are complete.

Gradually introduce your puppy to busier conditions. Mc puppies take everything in thei stride, enjoying their outings, meeting people, and, inevitabl receiving lots of attention.

If your puppy lacks confidence, slow down! Don't l him be intimidated by crowds o

Broaden your puppy's horizons by introducing a variety of different experiences.

ople or noisy traffic conditions. Keep to quieter areas for a
nger period, and then slowly introduce him to the busier
eas. Puppies can easily be frightened by experiencing too
uch too soon. This applies equally to the adult dog who has
en rehomed. Take things slowly, and give the dog time to
velop his confidence and his trust in you.

As the puppy gains experience, introduce him to other
nditions such as steps, and, if you live in an apartment,
evators, as well as public transportation. Vary the areas you
alk your puppy. Go to different parks and shops; all these
tivities will help with the temperamental development of
ur dog.

ther Dogs

is important that your puppy learns how to mix with other
gs. The best way of doing this is by attending a local puppy
ass. This will provide the opportunity to teach your puppy
behave in the company of other dogs. A rescued dog will
so benefit from this type of socialization, but you will need
attend a class for adult dogs.

If you already have an older dog at home, do not allow the
ppy to pester him continually.
though some adults
ll enjoy or tolerate
orief spell of play
th the puppy,
any will
ickly tire of
ugh puppy
havior and
ll end the
ssion by
tting the puppy
rmly in his place.

*Learning to mix with other dogs is
an essential part of growing up.*

11

Toys and Games

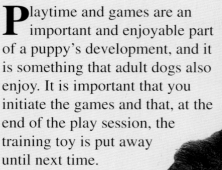

Playtime and games are an important and enjoyable part of a puppy's development, and it is something that adult dogs also enjoy. It is important that you initiate the games and that, at the end of the play session, the training toy is put away until next time.

Do not allo[w] your dog t[o] become possessive about toys.

You can teach your dog to give up a toy by offering a treat. As the dog spits the toy out, say "Give," pick up the toy, and then give the treat. Rewar[d] with stroking and verbal praise. Be consistent, and make sure you always give the command so that the response is automatic. Never allow your dog to snatch a toy from the handler.

Teach your dog to gi[ve] up his toy by exchanging it for a treat.

Playing with Children

Children and dogs can develop wonderful relationships, bu[t] it is essential that both puppy and child grow up respecting one another. Children should avoid playing games of strength, such as tug-of-war and wrestling, unless they are able to control the situation.

Play with your puppy often, but try not to exhaust him. Energetic, enthusiastic children can easily overexcite a puppy, resulting in rough play. The puppy will play with your child in exactly the same way he would play with another dog. This means using sharp claws and needle-sharp teeth—and, inevitably, the game ends in tears. The puppy has been allowed to become excitable and boisterous, and no puppy benefits from this type of encouragement.

Small children should be taught the following rules:

Leave the puppy alone when he is in his bed.
It is important for the puppy to have plenty of opportunity to rest and sleep without being disturbed. His bed should be a place of sanctuary. If the puppy is constantly disturbed, he may become anxious and could show signs of irritability.

Do not touch the puppy or interfere with his food bowl while he is eating.
The puppy could perceive any erratic behavior on the part of a child as a threat. This could lead to the puppy becoming overprotective of his food or his bowl.

Do not pick up the puppy or carry him.
Toddlers should sit on the floor and allow the puppy in their laps for a cuddle. This will preclude a small child from dropping the pup, and the pup learns not to jump up on the child.

Children and dogs must learn mutual respect.

The Collar and Lead

The lead is an important training aid in all situations. It can be used around the home and yard as well as for walking outside. Put your dog on the lead for all early learning sessions because this will ensure a more successful lesson. Your close proximity will give the dog confidence, you will be in control of the situation, and your dog will not be able to evade training interaction. Choose a lightweight collar and lead for this purpose.

First Steps

Introduce your puppy to a buckle collar while he is playing the yard, when he's eating, or at a time when you can observ him. Gradually extend the length of time you leave the colla on, over a period of two to three days. In most cases, the do; will scratch and complain for about five minutes, and will then give in and forget it is there.

Once your dog has accepted wearing a collar, condition hi to accept the lead by clipping it or for five to ten minutes and allowin it to trail. This should only be don during a supervised play session to ensure the lead does not get caugh on anything.

Occasionally pick up the lead ar crouch down, encouraging him to come to you. When he responds, praise and pet him. Repeat the exercise several times each sessio Practice this procedure in the backyard and around the house before venturing out into the neighborhood.

Lots of encouragement is needed in the early stages of lead training.

First Walks and Exercise

Most dogs usually accept wearing the lead and collar quite quickly. When they realize that the lead means a walk and new vistas to explore, they look forward to seeing it appear.

A patient, positive approach by the handler is required. Speak to your puppy frequently; verbal encouragement and praise will inspire the dog to walk at your side as you move along.

Avoid getting too far ahead of the dog, and never be tempted to drag or pull him. Use a toy or treat, or arrange for a friend to walk an experienced dog in front, to encourage forward movement.

Walking on the Lead (Heelwork)

The aim of most pet owners is to have a dog who will walk beside them without pulling. This is how to do it.

Place a chain or fabric training collar on the dog.

Position the dog on your left side and start off with your left foot.

With a treat, encourage the dog to stay even with your left knee.

Gently tighten the lead as he moves too fast or too slow.

When he has Heeled a few feet, stop and reward him with praise and a tidbit.

Stationary Exercises

The Sit

Don't forget to "train as your dog does!" This means that any time you see your puppy moving into the Sit position, give the "Sit" command.

In training sessions, follow these stages:

- Put your dog on the lead.
- Stand in front of your dog.
  - Hold the lead in your left hand, and have a tasty treat in your right hand.
  - Show your dog the treat, and quickly close it in your hand.
  - Move the treat toward your dog's nose but fractionally higher (this action should push your dog's head up and backward into his shoulders). As your dog follows the direction of the food, he will sit.
  - Give the command "Sit" as your dog lowers his bottom into position.
  - Immediately give the treat. Stroke and praise your dog in the Sit position, then release and play.
- Repeat the exercise.
- Practice the Sit response before feeding your dog and before you put him on the lead.

An adult dog should respond to the verbal command instantly.

If your dog keeps jumping up or nudging for the treat, do not pull your hand away. This will only encourage him to follow your hand. Hold the treat very still in a closed hand, be patient, and only reward for sitting still.

The Down

Apply "train as your dog does." Any time your puppy naturally moves into the Down position, give the "Down" command. When training the Down, put your dog on the lead.

Your dog should be on your left-hand side in the Sit position. Kneel beside your puppy.

With the lead and a treat in your right hand, place the thumb and first finger of your left hand immediately behind the dog's shoulder blades.

Using the treat, lure the dog's nose toward his chest, and then toward the ground at the point directly between his feet.

In order to get the treat, the dog will begin to collapse. At this point, apply very light pressure behind the shoulder blades (do not push, as this would cause resistance).

As the dog moves into a Down position, slowly draw the treat forward and give the command "Down."

Give the treat while gently stroking the dog with your left hand. Praise with a calm voice, give the release command and play.

Repeat the exercise.

Use a treat to lure the dog into the Down.

Apply light pressure on the shoulder blades to get the dog into the correct position.

Stationary Exercises

TRAINING TIP

Training should be done anywhere and everywhere—the kitchen, the family room, the hall, and the backyard are all good places to begin.

Do not allow your dog to creep forward to take the treat. If this happens, quickly push the treat toward the dog's nose, which will make him back off from your hand.

Remember that misuse of commands will create a poor response; e.g.,

"Sit down"—Which command do you mea the Sit or the Down?

"Get down"—Some people instinctively us this command when the dog jumps up. Try t use a completely different command for jumping up at people or furniture, such as "Get off."

The Stay

The "Stay" command can be used in conjunction with the Sit and the Down.

Stage One

• Once the dog is in the Sit or the Down position, use the "Stay" command. Count to five, then reward with a treat, release and play.

• Gradually increase the time of withholding the treat.

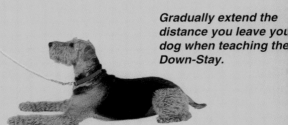

Gradually extend the distance you leave you dog when teaching the Down-Stay.

Second Stage

Now the handler must move position and gradually start to increase the distance between dog and handler.

Example I

Put the dog in the Down position, kneel beside him, and give the "Stay" command. Slowly stand up straight, repeating the "Stay" command. Hold the new position for a few seconds.
Kneel down again by your dog's side, praise in position, reward, release and play.

Example II

Put the dog in the Sit position, stand beside him and give the "Stay" command. Take one step to the right, repeating the "Stay" command. Hold the new position for a few seconds.
Return to your dog's side, praise in position, reward, release and play.
Stop using treats once you start to increase the distance of the Stay. The release and play should be sufficient reward if done enthusiastically.

The Wait

This is a very useful command. Use it when you want your dog to remain stationary for a short time. It is best described as a temporary "halt" before giving another command (e.g., when teaching recall or when opening a car or house door).

The Sit-Stay: Remember to reward your dog when the exercise has been completed.

TRAINING TIP

At the completion of a successful exercise, reward your dog and praise him in that position, then give a "release" command, such as "Finish" or "Okay."

Come

This is the most important and useful command you can eve
teach your dog. When you first get your dog home, "train as
the dog does," as often as possible. Whenever the dog
approaches you for attention or a cuddle, say: "Good
girl/boy, come." Stroke him first, and then reward with a
small treat.

Stage One

Formal early training for the
"Come" command should
always be carried out on a
long line. This should
measure 6–8 ft. in length.

• Hold the line and treat in
your right hand, show the
dog his treat, and slowly
back away.

• As the dog follows you,
give the command "Come."

• Keep repeating the
command over five to six
paces. Then stroke the dog
with your left hand, and give
the treat. Give lots of verbal
and physical praise.

• Keep the line short at this
stage, as this will enable you
to stop the puppy wandering
off or avoiding interaction.

*Stage One: Attach a training
line and call the dog to you as
you back off five or six paces*

Stage Two

Once a good response has been achieved in Stage One, you can progress to the next stage.

With your puppy on your left, tell him to "Sit" and "Wait." Keep the line loose, and with a treat in the right hand, slowly turn and face your dog.

Take one step backward, stand still. Now call your dog's name and say "Come."

Walk backward as the dog approaches, reeling in the lead at the same time. Stroke and then give the treat. Reward with verbal and physical praise.

Slowly increase the number of backward steps you take until you reach the end of the long line.

Stage Two: Tell the dog to "Wait," step back, gradually extending the distance, and call the dog in.

Stage Three

With your dog on your left, tell him to "Sit" and "Wait," and calmly place the long line on the floor beside your dog.

Turn and face your dog, repeat the "Wait" command, and back away a reasonable distance.

Stand still (extend the time your puppy Sits and Waits gradually), call his name, give the command "Come," stroke and reward.

Stage Three: Lay the training line on the ground, face the dog, and then call him in.

On the Move

Practice these three stages in different locations so your do
learns that, as with all commands, they apply in all situation

Introduce some distractions such as children playing or
leaving a favorite toy nearby. Training classes will provide
the opportunity to attempt the exercise when other dogs are
around.

Reward intermittently to avoid complacency. You will
achieve a more positive response if your dog does not know
he will receive a reward or not.

Your puppy is now ready to practice the "Come" response
in a park or field. Choose a safe environment, without
distractions or dangers, and be sure your dog is focused on
you.

Stage Four

Free-run your puppy
trailing the long line
to enable you to
reinforce the
"Come" if response
is poor. Once you
are confident that
you can achieve a
good response from
your puppy
regularly, remove
the long line to
practice off-lead
response.

Stage Four: Practi
off-leash recal

Puppies often go through a
"deaf" stage around six months
of age! If this happens, attach the long line again to remind
your dog that you are still in control, even at a distance, and
to reestablish the desired response.

The Retrieve

Most dogs enjoy retrieving—it is a useful game and it helps with recall training.

Attach a favorite toy to a lightweight long line. Play with your dog to establish interest and enthusiasm in the toy.

Throw the toy a short distance, and allow your dog to chase after and pick it up.

Now call the dog to you, verbally praising as he approaches you. Do not make a grab for the toy.

Physically praise your dog for at least thirty seconds before taking the toy away to throw it again.

The long line attached to the toy prevents the dog from running away with it.

Your dog should always enjoy coming back to you for that extra special praise you give before you take the toy away. If you fail to physically praise at this point, the dog will become reluctant to approach you holding the toy.

When your dog is returning the toy to you with enthusiasm, remove the long line.

First get your dog interested in the retrieve toy.

The dog runs out to get the toy—but the training line means the handler remains in control.

New Challenges

TRAINING TIP

To prevent fear of large groups of people, don't allow your puppy to be frightened by large boisterous crowds.

Dog Training Classes

You can teach all the basic training exercises at home, but both you and your dog will benefit from attending dog training classes. However, finding a good dog training club is not always easy. Contact as many different sources of information as possible. Try your veterinarian, pet shop, other dog owners, the local library, or community information center. The AKC or a local dog club can provide a list of training clubs.

Before deciding on a suitable club, visit several, without taking your dog, and observe the methods of training. If you do not like the way things are done, try another club. Avoid those that advocate the use of punishment or excessive force.

Most clubs will take puppies as soon as they have completed their full course of

Dogs love Agility, but you must be confident of having full control before attempting this discipline.

ccinations. Attending
ch classes should
able you to improve
responses and
neral behavior. The
structor should teach
u how to implement
e basic commands
d show you relevant
ndling techniques.
any all-breed clubs
rform Canine Good
tizen tests, which
aluate your dog's
sic obedience and
od manners.

*Competitive Obedience
requires accuracy,
precision—and a lot of
patience.*

pecialized Training

you want to improve your skills further,
ere are a variety of disciplines available,
ch as competitive Obedience, Agility, or
yball, and your instructor should be able to
vise you of a local club that specializes in
e field you wish to pursue.

Troubleshooting

Despite all your efforts, sometimes problems occur in training. If these are dealt with effectively, at an early stage, undesirable behavior can be corrected before the dog gets the upper hand in your relationship.

Problem 1: Jumping Up

My dog constantly jumps up at me, and at visitors when they first arrive in the house.

Jumping up can become a real problem.

Solutions

- Avoid touching the dog to push him off. Turn your back on him and do not make eye contact.
- Don't wait for your dog to jump up at you; counter-command him "Sit" as he approaches, and then praise him for doing so.
- Attach your dog to a long line. When you answer the door, allow the dog to go forward on a loose lead to greet the visitor. As soon as the dog attempts to jump up, take a step backward and correct, saying "No." Then immediately allow your dog to go forward again. The dog will learn that he is allowed to go forward and greet, but on your terms. The visitor must not acknowledge the dog when he jumps up.
- Encourage visitors to ignore the dog for a few minutes and greet you first instead.

Keep your dog on a lead or a training line, and command him to "Sit" before he is greeted.

Problem 2: Poor Recall

My dog ignores me, or returns very slowly, when I ask him to "Come" at the end of a walk.

Solutions

Is the bad habits of the owner that are usually the cause for the breakdown in the "Come" response.

Never call him to you to scold, and never scold him for or response. Instead,

Practice the "Come" response throughout the free run, so your dog never anticipates when he is going to be put back on the lead.

Remember to use the word "Come." All too often, a handler calls the dog's name, but does not tell him what to do! Always reward your dog for returning to you, even if you have not called him.

Problem 3: Dog Aggression

My dog is aggressive toward other dogs that we meet when we are out on walks.

Solutions

Allow plenty of early socialization with other dogs

Practice recalls throughout a free run, so your dog does not anticipate the end of the walk—and the end of his freedom.

If you plan to leave your dog on his own, or you want him to settle down because you are expecting visitors, a short training session is more likely to achieve tiredness than a free run or a walk.

as your dog grows up. Always praise good behavior with other dogs.

• Protect your dog from obviously aggressiv dogs. Avoid confrontation, cross the road, o change route in the park, if necessary.

• If your dog is growling at another dog, never stroke him or pick him up. This action will be perceived by your dog as praise of unacceptable behavior. Ignore the behavior and walk away and then call your dog to yo Do not start shouting and interfering. Most dogs will sort out their differences more quickly and more easily if you don't get involved.

• If you meet another dog when your dog is the lead, continually speak to your dog and retain his focus on you Once the dogs have greeted each other, wa on, encouraging him to keep the lead slack. Reward your dog with tidbit when he has walked away and his concentration is once again on you.

Dogs that are used to socializing from an early age will rarely become aggressive with other dog

roblem 4: The orried Dog

y dog seems worried when angers come to the house.

olutions

o not coax your dog to et strangers. Avoid using ise, such as "Good girl," to courage a more confident tude—all you will be doing raising shyness. Ignore the havior and concentrate on visitor.

ncourage visitors to ignore dog. They should not ke eye contact with the , talk to him, or try to ich him. Most importantly, not allow visitors to pursue dog.

efore you answer the door, ich your dog to a long line. is will increase his level of nfidence. Ask your dog to , and do not force him ward to greet visitors. ntrol any barking with a irp "No." Once the visitors in the house, allow the dog rail the line and move und freely. If the dog roaches a visitor, he should

Do not force a worried dog to greet visitors.

Wait until the dog is ready to make an approach; then reward with a treat.

be ignored. Once the dog has voluntarily approached the visitor two or three times, th visitor should offer a tasty treat. Reward the dog for approaching, not for backing off or running away.

• The dog will quickly gain confidence if the visitor avoids eye contact and resists trying t touch the dog.

Problem 5: Destructive Behavior

My dog is very destructive, particularly when he is left on his own.

Solutions

• Ensure that your dog is mentally tired before leaving him. A short training session will achieve this.

• Leave your dog with something to do. A nylon bone will keep him occupied.

• Give him an old item of your clothing. This will act as a comforter in your absence

• Practice leaving your dog for short periods—five minutes at a time to star with. Gradually increa

Destructive behavio can be caused by boredom or by anxiety.

period of time he is left alone.
member to reward good
havior.

ry to make your departures
d arrivals as uneventful as
ssible. Don't make a big issue
going out.

Unless you catch your dog in
e act of chewing, never scold
n on your return. You might
nk he knows what he has done
cause he is cringing in the
rner, but, in fact, he is only
ponding to your
dy language and
gry voice.

nvest in an indoor
te. These are very
od for teaching your dog to
tle down while you are out.
ur dog may be in need of a more secure
ting place, and the correct use of an indoor
te can provide this.

ally, remember that it is your responsibility
give your dog the confidence and training
behave in an acceptable manner. Ninety-
e percent of dogs are eager to please;
ety-nine percent of owners will end up
th the dog they deserve!

*Try to make
departures and
arrivals uneventful so
your dog does not
become worried.*